BELIEVING IN ME

Originally published by Summersdale Publishers Ltd. as *You're A Star* in London, England, 2018.

First Skyhorse edition, 2019.

Sky Pony Press books may be purchased in bulk at special discounts for sales promotion, corporate gifts, fund-raising, or educational purposes. Special editions can also be created to specifications. For details, contact the Special Sales Department, Sky Pony Press, 307 West 36th Street, 11th Floor, New York, NY 10018 or info@skyhorsepublishing.com.

Sky Pony® is a registered trademark of Skyhorse Publishing, Inc.®, a Delaware corporation.

Visit our website at www.skyponypress.com.

10 9 8 7 6 5

Manufactured in China, January 2024
This product conforms to CPSIA 2008

Library of Congress Cataloging-in-Publication Data is available on file.

Text by Poppy O'Neill
Interior and cover design by Summersdale Publishers Ltd.

Print ISBN: 978-1-5107-4747-0

Printed in China

BELIEVING IN ME

A Child's Guide to Self-Confidence and Self-Esteem

Poppy O'Neill
Foreword by Amanda Ashman-Wymbs

Sky Pony Press
New York

★ CONTENTS ★

FOREWORD

Amanda Ashman-Wymbs, Counsellor and Psychotherapist, registered and accredited by the British Association for Counselling and Psychotherapy

Having the experience of raising two daughters and working with many young people therapeutically, it is clear to me that issues of self-esteem impact strongly on the health and well-being of young people today. Enabling children to gain awareness of and understand their inner world, and finding ways and tools to establish or re-establish a healthy relationship with themselves, are invaluable both to support their current everyday experience and also to allow them to establish healthy patterns which they can take into their adolescence and adult life.

Believing in Me by Poppy O'Neill is a fantastic workbook, written in a simple way, with fun characters and exercises that will appeal to children and help them to understand what self-esteem is. It introduces exercises which allow children to gain awareness of their emotions and thought processes, and enables and encourages them to see clearly and focus on the strengths and resources that they already have within themselves, as well as supporting them to try new behaviors in small manageable steps. This book helps children to understand and value their own and everyone else's uniqueness, as well as supporting them to identify what true friendships are and are not. It explores vital factors such as body image and covers the importance of having a healthy lifestyle for well-being. There is also an introduction to gentle meditation and mindfulness practices, which allows direct connection with present-moment experiences through the body and senses, thus enabling children to get to know and learn how to easily access the resource of peace and happiness that is always within them.

I highly recommend this book as a very effective tool which parents can use to help support children to understand themselves better, and to work through and transcend difficulties with confidence and self-esteem, allowing them to fully shine as who they are.

INTRODUCTION: A GUIDE FOR PARENTS AND CARERS

You're not alone

This practical guide combines proven cognitive-behavioral therapy methods used by child psychologists with simple activities to help your child to grow their self-esteem. You may have noticed that your child seems a little more reserved than other children or they don't want to be involved in activities because they don't think they're "good enough." Sometimes it doesn't matter how encouraging you are, you just can't get them to believe in themselves, and that's the thing about self-esteem—it's not about how others see you, it's about how you see yourself.

This book is aimed at children aged 8–12 years—a lot happens in these years that can impact a child's sense of self-worth, not just now but for years to come. Close friendships form, it will be the first time their knowledge and skills are tested in exams, they develop a greater awareness of their physical selves and begin to compare their attractiveness to others. They may also begin to use social media and encounter peer pressure for the first time and they can experience the early stages of puberty and its accompanying mood swings. It's hardly surprising, therefore, that there may be times when they struggle with the challenges of growing up and for some children this can affect their self-esteem.

So if you feel that your child may be suffering from low self-esteem, rest assured that you are not alone.

Signs of low self-esteem

To help determine if your child has low self-esteem, look out for these signs. They may manifest as your child begins to relate to the world around them, be it in everyday or specific situations:

- They are self-critical, saying things such as, "I'm no good at this," "Everyone is better than me," etc.

- They avoid challenges because they think they will fail

- They struggle to accept praise or criticism and are particularly sensitive to others' opinions of them

- They lose interest in school and succeeding because they don't think they "measure up" to their peers

- They experience mood swings

- They are strongly influenced by peer pressure

- They can become controlling to disguise their feelings of powerlessness and low self-worth

Keep a diary to help you find out if you notice these behaviors at specific times so that you're better equipped to help your child if there's a particular issue, such as an activity that they're struggling with or a person who might be causing them upset.

The important thing to remember is it's never too late to start helping your child to boost their self-esteem.

Talking it over

What you say to your child—and how you say it—has a huge influence on how they see themselves. When your child has low self-esteem you can sometimes feel that you should give them more compliments to give them a boost, but complimenting your child too often and for minor achievements can encourage them to lower their standards in order to feel better about themselves.

It's important to recognize that overcompensating for your child's low self-esteem by overly praising them can't make a situation better. To solve a problem you need to find out the causes and accurately identify the issue at hand: communicate with your child and talk about a specific issue when it arises. Are they struggling with maths? Has someone been mean to them in class? Perhaps they feel they are less attractive than someone else? Allow them to express how they feel and help your child to take positive steps to begin solving their problems. Offer your support and be there for them, guiding them through their problems and helping them to reach solutions. Your child needs to learn how to deal with a problem and master the negative feelings that accompany it in order to grow into a confident person with healthy self-esteem.

Getting started: How to use this book

Guide your child through the activities in this book—just one at a time, perhaps once a week or every few days. Allow your child to set the pace and work on the activities independently—this is important because by developing your child's independence you are simultaneously building their self-esteem. The activities are designed to get them thinking about themselves and to grow their self-esteem by helping them to recognize and appreciate their strengths and uniqueness, and what makes them special. When your child feels good about themselves they are better equipped to deal with the challenges of everyday life. Make them aware that they have your support and help them to learn successful habits to deal with their problems independently, then watch their self-esteem soar.

Hopefully this book will be helpful for you and your child, enabling greater understanding of what self-esteem is and how to increase a sense of self-worth and confidence. However, if you have any serious concerns about your child's mental health that aren't addressed in the book, your GP is the best person to go to for further advice.

HOW TO USE THIS BOOK: A GUIDE FOR CHILDREN

This book is for you if you often…

★   Feel like you're not good enough compared to others

★   Think you won't do well enough or you will fail at something

★   Don't feel like you want to try your best

★   Miss out on fun activities because you think something will go wrong

If that sounds like you sometimes, or all of the time, this book is here to help. How you feel about yourself can change and you have the power to change it for the better! Inside you'll find some ideas to guide you and activities to help you see yourself in a positive way, feel braver and be more confident.

There might be things in the book you want to talk about with a trusted adult. That could be your mom or dad, your carer, one of your teachers, a big brother or sister, grandparent, aunt, uncle, next-door neighbor, or any other adult that you know well and feel comfortable talking to.

You can read through it at your own pace, no need to rush. This book is about you, so there are no wrong answers! You are the expert on you and this book is the perfect place to write all those things down.

Are you ready? Then let's begin.

INTRODUCING BOP THE MONSTER

Hello, I'm Bop and I'm here to guide you through this book. There are loads of activities and games to play, as well as some great ideas to read about. So, let's get cracking!

PART 1: WHAT IS SELF-ESTEEM?

How do you feel about yourself?

This is probably a question you've never really thought about but sometimes it helps to make time to do this. You may have heard people, especially grown-ups, talk about something called "self-esteem". Self-esteem is not something you can see or touch, but you can feel it and it's very powerful. So what is it? Self-esteem is the way you feel about yourself. Your self-esteem can be high or low, depending on how you feel. If you feel good about yourself and you are confident in your abilities, that's high self-esteem. If you feel bad about yourself and don't feel confident in your abilities, that's low self-esteem. Everyone feels bad about themselves sometimes, but when you do, it's important to think about solving the problem of why you are feeling bad and then moving on from it so you can feel happy again. Sometimes this is easier said than done, but this book will help you discover the ways to stay feeling good and show you how to develop ways to cope with things that get you down.

ACTIVITY: ALL ABOUT ME

Let's begin by finding out a bit more about you and your likes and dislikes. Fill in the spaces in the boxes below.

My name is...

Three words that describe me are...

When I grow up I would like to be...

I'm really good at...

My family members are...

For fun I like to...

ACTIVITY: WHAT MAKES ME GREAT!

Even if you're feeling down, you're still special and unique, and this activity invites you to give yourself a high-five for being so awesome. In each of the bubbles below, write down or draw something that you're good at or like about yourself:

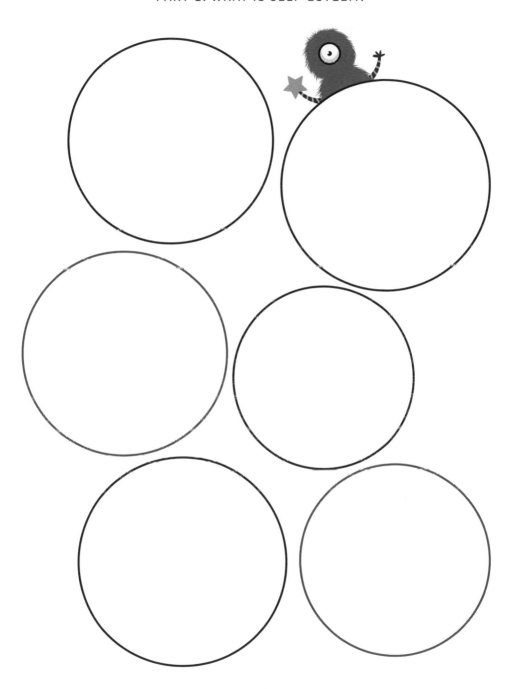

ACTIVITY: MY TREASURE BOX

What's important to you? Can you draw or write about the people you love, the things you enjoy and what you work hard at:

What are emotions?

Emotion is another word for a feeling. The four main emotions are:

* Happiness
* Fear
* Sadness
* Anger

But there are lots more! We feel emotions in our bodies, and they can feel small and quiet or big and loud. Some feelings feel good, and some feel bad.

Everyone has feelings, even if they don't always show them.

When you are feeling an emotion, it can feel like the emotion is taking over your whole body, which can lead to you having emotions and thoughts that are not very nice.

It's OK to feel whatever you are feeling, even if it's sad or angry. Feelings do change, and don't have to stick around for ages. Feelings pass through your body like a cloud passes through the sky.

ACTIVITY: HOW DO YOU FEEL RIGHT NOW?

Can you think of a way of describing or drawing your feeling? Maybe you can imagine it as weather (it could be sunny, cloudy, rainy), or as a shape, or you might even think of it as a color, an animal or alien? Have a go at describing or drawing how you feel in a way that makes the best sense to you.

I feel...

Now that you have a picture of your emotion, can you imagine yourself sitting next to it? Quietly watch and listen to the emotion and see what happens.

Drawing or describing your emotion helps you understand what you are feeling. If you've drawn a happy picture with a big yellow sun, you're likely to be feeling happy right now—why not turn to page 73 and start a Happy Jar?

If your drawing is of something frightening or unhappy, like a storm cloud, you're probably feeling bad in some way. Now is a good time to talk to a trusted grown-up about how you're feeling.

ACTIVITY: MEDITATION

Meditation is a way of making your brain be quiet and it's an activity you can try to help you feel calm. You can do it anywhere, but a quiet, comfy chair in your house or a shady spot outside are good places to try it out.

* Set a timer for five minutes, or choose a relaxing song to listen to (when you get to the end of the song you'll know you have completed the exercise)

* Sit comfortably

* Close your eyes

* Think about your breathing, how each breath in feels, and then how your breath out feels. Don't hold your breath but try to slowly breathe in through your nose, then slowly breathe out through your nose—as you do this, listen to the sound of your breath. The idea is that if you focus on the sound and feeling of your breath going in and out of your nose your brain doesn't have time to think about other stuff

* If other thoughts come into your mind, don't worry, just bring your thoughts back to your breath, in and out

* When the timer goes or the music finishes, open your eyes slowly

How did meditation make you feel? Circle or color in your feelings below:

Relaxed   Happy

                                        Bored

                    Upset

Hungry   Sleepy

                                Worried

            Silly

Curious

                                        Peaceful

★ **Meditating might feel strange at first, but if you keep practising you'll find it's a really useful way to help you feel calm.**

I CAN TAKE A DEEP BREATH

Signs of high and low self-esteem

Having high self-esteem feels like this:

* ★ Being happy

* ★ Feeling that you're a good person

* ★ Believing in yourself

* ★ Looking forward to a good future

* ★ Enjoying the world around you

* ★ Feeling energetic and hopeful

* ★ Feeling confident that you have the power to change things in your life

* ★ Joining in with others

* ★ Being happy with each good thing that happens, no matter how small

* ★ Looking for ways to do well

* ★ Encouraging others

* ★ Respecting others' differences and your own

* ★ Accepting that you will make mistakes and you can learn from them

But having low self-esteem feels like this:

* ★ Feeling unhappy

* ★ Feeling that you are not as good as others in some way

* ★ Having no confidence in yourself

* ★ Feeling hopeless about the future

* ★ Seeing the bad things in the world around you

* ★ Feeling like bad things always happen to you

* ★ Feeling tired most of the time

* ★ Sitting about and not doing anything active

* ★ Putting yourself down even when someone is giving you a compliment

* ★ Looking on the worst side of everything

* ★ Having no respect for yourself

ACTIVITY: RATE YOUR SELF-ESTEEM

Everyone's self-esteem is different, and it can go up and down depending on how you feel or what you're doing at a particular moment.

Where is your self-esteem right now? Draw an arrow on the gauge where you think it is:

low

I CAN TALK ABOUT
MY FEELINGS

PART 2: BOOSTING SELF-ESTEEM

Now that we've learned what high and low self-esteem feel like, let's look at ways to put low self-esteem in the bin and start feeling excellent about ourselves.

low self-esteem

THERE IS ONLY
ONE ME

ACTIVITY: WHAT MAKES YOU FEEL GOOD?

Everyone has different things that can make them feel high or low self-esteem. Write or draw yours below—you can include as many or as few as you like.

High: what makes me feel good about myself
E.g., being with my best friend, riding my bike

Can you do one of these things every day?

ACTIVITY: WHAT MAKES YOU FEEL BAD?

Low: what makes me feel bad about myself
E.g., being left out, a tricky school subject

**It's normal for things to make us experience low self-esteem sometimes.
Keep going—in the next chapter we'll look at ways to tackle these feelings.**

ACTIVITY: LISTEN TO YOUR THOUGHTS

What are you thinking about right now? Take a moment to notice the thoughts in your head. Try writing your thoughts like this:

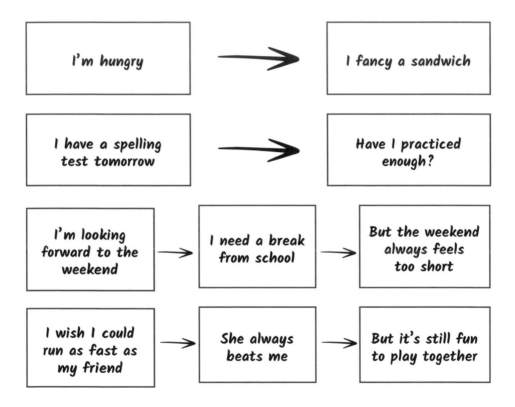

Sometimes just writing something down can make you feel better. It's almost like you're moving the thoughts from your head to the piece of paper. Once you've written something you can keep it, show it to someone you trust, or screw it up and throw it in the bin.

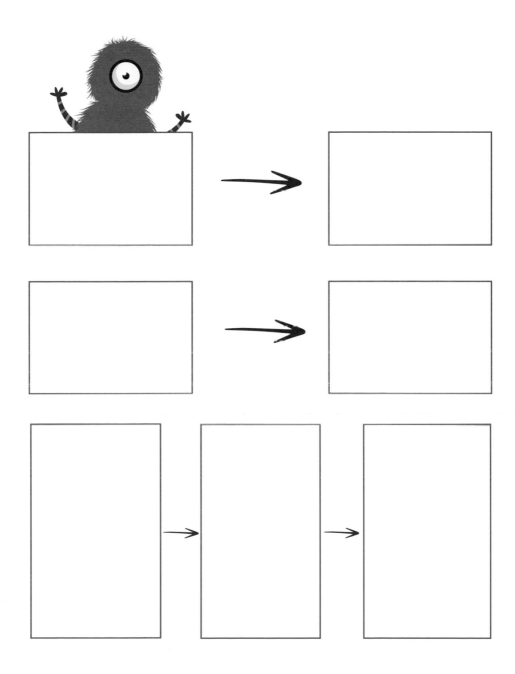

Mindfulness

Mindfulness is a practice that started in a spiritual movement called Buddhism. It means paying attention to what is happening and how we feel at this exact moment.

Being mindful can help us feel calmer and is a great way to deal with big or complicated feelings. Lots of people use mindfulness every day, and if you're experiencing low self-esteem, mindfulness is a great way to help you feel peaceful, calm and free.

Try it!

You can use mindfulness any time! Just take a moment to notice the things around you, what you are thinking and how you are feeling.

Here are a few ideas to get you started:

★ **Close your eyes and put one hand on your tummy. Breathe deeply and concentrate on your hand moving up and down with your breath.**

★ **When you are eating, try to notice all the flavors and textures as you taste and feel them on your tongue. Notice how your tummy feels after eating.**

> ★ When it's raining, take a moment to feel the raindrops on your skin. Are the drops cold? Are they big and fat or tingling drizzle?

> ★ Stand barefoot and concentrate on the ground or floor under your feet. Can you feel its texture? Is it warm or cold? Soft or hard? What other words could you use to describe it?

Hopefully these exercises will help you feel calm and more in control of your emotions. Just like anything else, the more you practise mindfulness, the easier and more useful it will become!

THOUGHTS ARE ONLY THOUGHTS — THEY AREN'T FACTS

Self-esteem boost

What can you do when your self-esteem is low?

- ★ Go outside, whatever the weather: watch how the trees move, smell the air, jump in a puddle, collect some interesting leaves

- ★ Smile—even if you don't feel happy, scientists have found that smiling can make you feel better

- ★ Put your books in alphabetical order or arrange them by color

- ★ Go to the park with a parent/carer

- ★ Make some art—you could draw, paint or collage, use fuse beads, chalk, cardboard—use your imagination!

- ★ Do some exercise, like star jumps or cycling

- ★ Listen to happy or relaxing music

- ★ Draw

- ★ Read

We are all different!

Every single human being on planet earth is different. From what we eat for breakfast to what we are scared of, no two people are the same.

Some differences you can see, and some you can't.

Most differences that can be seen from the outside don't tell us anything about the kind of person we are inside. Just because Bop is hairy, doesn't mean Bop needs to like the same things or have the same thoughts as other hairy monsters.

Some differences can feel big because we can see them clearly.

Boys and girls, people with freckles and people without, people with disabilities and people without, people with curly hair and people with straight hair. Our bodies are a little different, that's all. Each person has their own special way of being themselves.

ACTIVITY: YOUR FRIENDS

Think about one of your good friends—what do you have in common with them? What is different? Draw or write about you and your friend here:

E.g., Hair color, favorite TV show, best subject at school

How to spot a true friend

True friends are brilliant. They are the people we love to be with most in the world. However, sometimes, someone who says they are your friend can be someone you don't like to spend time with, maybe even someone who bullies you.

Just because someone spends time with you and says they are your friend, doesn't make it true! False friends are like bullies in disguise. Low self-esteem can sometimes mean we put up with unkind treatment from people who are supposed to be our friends, but remember: you don't have to spend time with people who are unkind to you or make you feel bad about yourself.

A true friend:

★ Listens to you

★ Talks to you kindly

★ Stands up for you

★ Includes you

★ Makes you feel good about yourself

A false friend:

★ Ignores you

★ Leaves you out

★ Hurts you

★ Teases or embarrasses you

★ Makes you feel bad about yourself

Important
★ If you are being bullied, it's important to remember that it's not your fault. Talk to a trusted adult about what is happening. You are important and you deserve to be treated with respect.

ACTIVITY: WHAT KIND OF FRIEND AM I?

Having good friends around helps boost self-esteem, and so does remembering all the ways you're a brilliant friend too!

Fill in the blank badges below with examples of how you are a good friend, e.g., "I am a good listener," then you can cut out your badges (but be careful) and use them to decorate your diary, or stick them to some cardboard, add a peg or safety pin and wear them!

I AM MY OWN PERSON, NOT BETTER OR WORSE THAN ANYONE ELSE

> **Better out than in**
>
> ★ Thoughts have a habit of filling up our heads, which can get noisy, especially when there are lots of different thoughts all trying to get your attention!
>
> ★ Keep a notebook with you so you can write down any thoughts that are getting too noisy. Once they are in the notebook, they can escape from your head.

ACTIVITY: I'M A STAR!

You're awesome: remind yourself why!

Can you finish these sentences?

I was proud when I...

Today I did well at...

I'm looking forward to...

I have fun when...

What can affect my self-esteem?

Before we move on to ways of controlling your unhappy thoughts, let's look in more detail at how self-esteem works. Lots of things can affect self-esteem, including:

* ★ Past experiences that leave you with happy or sad memories (like a fun holiday, or a time you were bullied)

* ★ The actions and words of others (like when a teacher says "well done" for a piece of work, or when a friend ignores you)

* ★ Our own thoughts (like when you think "I can do this!" or "this is too hard, I'm scared to try")

How can we solve the problem of low self-esteem?

By changing the way we think about ourselves and the world around us we can start to raise our self-esteem. If you can start to think more positively, you will start to feel more positive too.

Where does self-esteem come from?

Self-esteem comes from inside. Having high self-esteem means believing in yourself even when upsetting things happen. Having low self-esteem means seeing yourself in a negative way, and not being able to enjoy good things when they happen to you.

Can you help work out where Bop's self-esteem comes from?

The teacher has asked Bop to stand up and read a story out loud to the rest of the class. Bop feels worried about making a mistake.

If Bop is experiencing high self-esteem, Bop's thoughts would go something like this:

If Bop is experiencing low self-esteem, Bop's thoughts might go like this:

Bop is worried the words will come out wrong and the other children will laugh… Bop doesn't want to do it! Bop is experiencing low self-esteem right now.

Where does Bop's low self-esteem come from? Is it…

A Bop's teacher

B The other children

C How Bop thinks about the situation, and what Bop is imagining will happen

The answer is C! Bop is feeling bad and afraid of trying, because Bop is imagining bad things will happen.

If I try, bad things will happen. I'd better not try.

So how can we boost Bop's self-esteem?

A Never ask Bop to read in class

B Put socks in the children's mouths so it's impossible for them to laugh at Bop

C Change the way Bop thinks and feels about reading aloud

It's C again! If Bop doesn't read at all, Bop's self-esteem won't get a chance to grow. It'll stay right where it is, or even get lower. Also, putting socks in children's mouths is mean!

In the next chapter we're going to look at ways to grow your self-esteem and keep it high by changing how you think, feel and act.

PART 3: CONTROLLING UNHAPPY THOUGHTS

We all have a little voice in our minds that tells us about ourselves. When you have high self-esteem, this little voice is kind and fair, but if you're feeling low in self-esteem, the voice can be unkind and make us believe untrue things about ourselves.

You have the power to change how this little voice talks to you.

What are my unhappy thoughts?

The first step in beating unhappy thoughts is working out what yours are. Below is a list of unhappy thoughts—tick any that you believe about yourself.

Unhappy thought	
Nobody likes me	☐
I'm boring	☐
I'm ugly	☐
I always fail	☐
Bad things always happen to me	☐
I need to be perfect to be happy	☐
If people get to know me, they won't like me	☐
I'm a bad person	☐

ACTIVITY: TRUE OR FALSE?

Now we're going to be detectives. Pick one of the unhappy thoughts you chose on the last page. We're going to look for facts to prove it wrong!

To help with this activity, you can ask yourself these questions:

★ Am I being fair to myself? E.g., It's not fair to think I should be perfect

★ Is it helpful to me to think this? E.g,. It's not helpful to think I am going to fail before I have tried

★ Is it likely that it's true? E.g., It's not likely that my friends all secretly dislike me

★ Is it based on facts? E.g., "I'm ugly" is not a fact

★ What facts prove this thought wrong?

★ Would I say it to my best friend?

You could present your investigation in a table like this one.

Thought	Prove it wrong!	Is the thought true?
I'm boring	I have good friends who enjoy spending time with me	No!

SOMETIMES I FEEL SAD, AND THAT'S OK. I CAN DO SOMETHING TO CHANGE MY FEELINGS.

Past experiences

Sometimes unhappy thoughts come from nowhere, and sometimes they come from past experiences.

If something has gone wrong when you tried before, you might think it will happen again. It can be very hard to find the courage to try again.

The truth is, no one gets everything right the first time. Everyone starts as a beginner, and the more times you practise, the easier and more enjoyable something will be.

How to respond to unhappy thoughts

Unhappy thoughts can be changed into hopeful ones, you just need to learn how!

Unhappy thoughts can come at any time to ruin your day, so we're going to learn how to fight them, and flip them into hopeful thoughts.

Take your unhappy thought and use positive self-talk to flip it into a hopeful one. Are you ready?

Thought mix-ups

Low self-esteem can develop when our brains react to bad feelings by panicking and mixing up thoughts. This is called a **thinking error**, and there are lots of different types…

Bop is having some thought mix-ups:

All-or-nothing thinking: if something isn't perfect, I've failed completely

Over-generalising: if one thing goes wrong, everything will go wrong

Focus on the negatives: if one thing goes wrong despite other things going right, that's the only thing I can think about

Fortune-telling: I know I'll fail

Mind-reading: I know everyone thinks badly of me

Catastrophe thinking: one mistake will ruin everything

Magnified thinking: The things I dislike about myself are the most important things about me. The things I like about myself aren't important

Negative comparison: my friend is better than me in every way

Unrealistic expectations: I should be perfect at everything

Putting yourself down: I'm a failure

Blaming yourself: everything goes wrong and it's all my fault

Feelings are facts: I feel ugly, so I must *be* ugly

Blaming others: if only people were nicer to me, I would be a better person

Do any of these sound like the voice
you talk to yourself with?
Draw a circle round any thoughts you recognize.

WHEN YOU SEE YOURSELF IN THE MIRROR, SAY SOMETHING NICE

Flip your thoughts!

There is more than one way of thinking about everything, and changing how you think helps to change your self-esteem.

* Bop the monster wants to learn a bicycle trick, but is finding it difficult. Bop sees a friend whizzing past, having loads of fun and thinks: *This is stupid, I'll never get it right—I give up!*

* Bop is scared to try in case the trick isn't perfect straight away. What Bop didn't see was their friend wobbling and falling off when they were first learning the trick

* Bop could give up, and miss out on having fun and learning something new

* Or, Bop could turn the unhappy thought into a hopeful one: *I can keep trying, and ask my friend for help if I need it*

Flip unhappy thoughts into hopeful thoughts!

The secret to flipping unhappy thoughts into hopeful ones is to think about solving the problem. Here's how you do it:

What I say	What I really think	Flip it!
This is stupid	I don't understand	I can ask for help
This is boring	It might be tricky	I can try one part at a time
I can't do it	I'm scared I won't be able to do it	I can try my best and ask for help
I'm bad at this	I tried before and wasn't perfect	I can practise and each time I do, it will get easier
This will take too long	This is too much for me	I can make a plan and work through it
This is too hard, I give up!	I feel bad that I can't do this perfectly right now	I can take a break and try again when I feel calmer

ACTIVITY: MY HOPEFUL THOUGHTS

Now it's your turn! Each time an unhappy thought tries to stop you from doing something, write it down here. Can you work out why you're thinking it? How can you turn it into a hopeful thought? (Don't forget you can look at the previous page to give yourself some help.)

If you get stuck, try imagining your best friend has come to you with the problem: what advice would you give?

What I say	What I really think	Flip it!

IT'S OK TO STRUGGLE SOMETIMES, AND IT'S OK TO FEEL WHAT I'M FEELING

ACTIVITY: BREAK IT DOWN

Sometimes things can seem very complicated, but once you break them down into small steps you'll see that they are actually made up of lots of easier steps that all work together towards an end goal.

Try drawing Bop the monster using these step-by-step instructions.

Step one:

Step two:

Step three:

Step four:

Step five:

Most of us have challenges in life that we think are too hard, like doing a tricky sum or reading a long but interesting book. Can you think of something that seems like it's going to be difficult? How could you break it down like the picture?

Keep a diary

★ It can be difficult to see all our unhappy thoughts at once, so try keeping a feelings diary. It can be secret if you like, so don't be afraid to write everything you're thinking and feeling. Try to write at least one positive thing each time you write in your diary, but don't be afraid to be honest if you're feeling low. Writing things down is a good way of organizing your thoughts, especially if you have a lot of tricky things to think about. Ask your parent to give you a notebook that you can write in to help with this. It needn't be a diary with dates in—you can add those yourself whenever you want to write in it.

I AM GOOD ENOUGH

ACTIVITY: MY HAPPY JAR

What makes you happy? We can find happiness in big or small things. The sound of the sea in a shell, a hug from someone special, remembering a fun birthday party… write as many happy things as you can think of on slips of paper. There are two below to get you started.

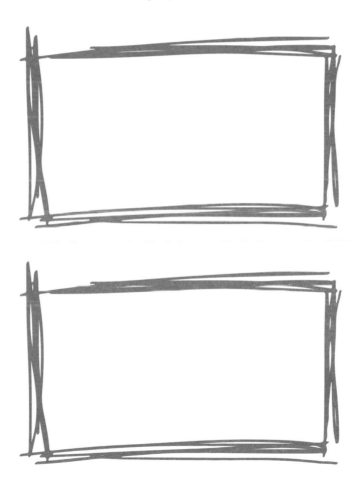

Now cut them out (be careful when doing this), fold them in half and keep them in an empty jar or a special box (you could even decorate your box with a happy design). Each time something good happens—big or small—write it down and put it in the jar with your other happy things.

Any time you feel down, take a piece of paper from the jar and it will give you a little boost of happiness.

Be kind to yourself

Just like anything else, thinking positively can be tricky at first. Don't feel bad when you have an unhappy thought, it doesn't mean you've failed. Everyone has them, even people who seem happy and confident all the time. Each time a negative thought pops up, see it as an opportunity to practise thinking hopefully and before you know it, you'll be an expert.

Let negative thoughts pass through your head like clouds or bubbles, then let them float away.

Change your behaviors

We all act and react to certain situations in different ways: these actions are called behaviors. To keep your self-esteem high and your brain and body feeling good, it's important to learn how to spot unhelpful behaviors and how to behave differently. Once you're in charge of your thoughts and how you behave, you'll be in control of your self-esteem too.

Unhelpful behaviors can keep your self-esteem low, and in this section we'll go through ways to change these unhelpful behaviors.

Some activities might seem scary at first, but everything can be broken down into small steps you can do at your own pace. Changing your self-esteem is hard work and can't be rushed. You're doing amazingly well already and should be very proud of yourself!

Taking small steps

The key to doing things that scare you is to take small steps. When Bop thinks about reading aloud in class, Bop's tummy aches with worry. So Bop breaks up the worry into steps, and finds a small step to start with:

★ First, Bop reads the book alone, quietly. It feels a bit scary at first because this is the book Bop is worried about reading aloud, but reading it quietly alone isn't too bad. After a few goes, Bop feels comfy reading it alone and quietly

★ Next, Bop reads alone, out loud. That feels a little odd to begin with, but quickly starts to feel OK

★ Bop then asks a grown-up to sit and listen while Bop reads the book. Bop has trouble with a few words, but carries on and does really well!

★ Bop still feels worried about reading aloud to the class, so Bop decides to read standing up in front of the grown-up. This feels uncomfortable so Bop tries again sitting down, then goes back to standing up

★ Bop asks the teacher to listen to the book being read out loud. Bop sits next to the teacher in the classroom and reads the book in a confident voice

★ Now Bop feels ready to read aloud, with the whole class listening. Bop still feels a little nervous, so chooses one page to read. Bop feels so proud!

Here are Bop's steps:

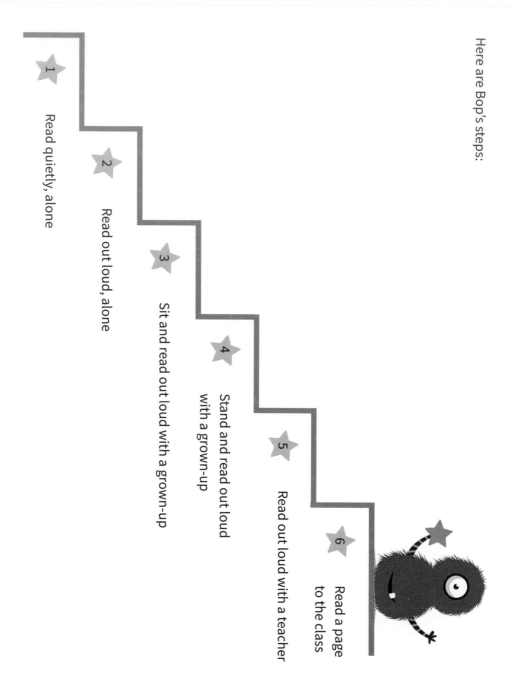

1 Read quietly, alone

2 Read out loud, alone

3 Sit and read out loud with a grown-up

4 Stand and read out loud with a grown-up

5 Read out loud with a teacher

6 Read a page to the class

ACTIVITY: SMALL STEPS

Can you draw or write the steps you could take to solve a problem you have? Make the first step something you feel comfy doing. For example, if you want to join a sports team, you could start by practising that sport in your garden. Use the diagram on the next page to help you.

Remember: you can stay on a step for as long as you need to! If you get stuck, ask a grown-up to help you.

> ⌃ **Different problems need different solutions, but the key to solving problems and growing your self-esteem is to take small steps.**

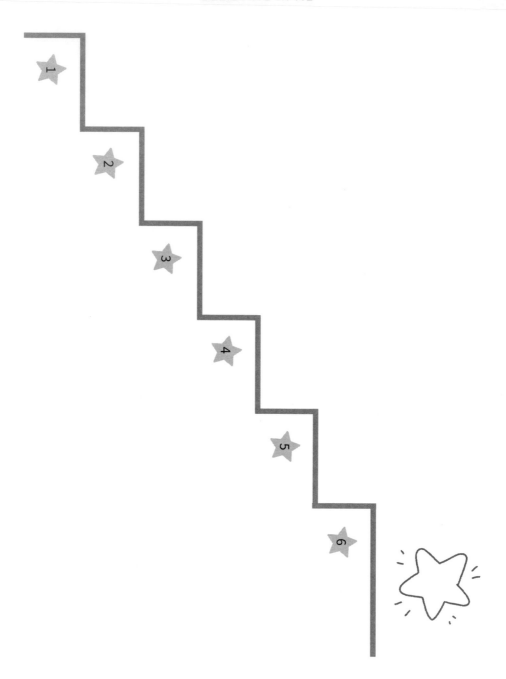

MY BEST IS
BEST FOR ME

Unhelpful behaviors

Thought mix-ups lead to unhappy thinking, which make us feel bad about ourselves. To hide these bad feelings, we sometimes behave in ways that make us feel safe for a little while, but that are not helpful to growing self-esteem. On the next few pages you'll find examples of these behaviors, as well as a note of where to find the solutions. Try to read about each behavior before you skip to the solution.

Avoidance: Hiding from or choosing not to do something because it challenges you.

Rosie would love to go to soccer club but she's worried the other children will laugh at her while she's learning how to play, so she chooses not to go at all.

Hiding: Keeping the things that make us different a secret from others.

Yusuf likes reading and writing poetry. He thinks his friends would laugh if they found out, so he keeps his hobby a secret.

Perfectionist: Trying to be perfect at everything you do.

Alex has no time to relax at the weekends because he spends all his spare time doing homework and chores. He thinks he will fail at school and his family and friends won't like him if he isn't brilliant at everything.

Passive: Trying to please others all the time, and not feeling able to say "no" to things you don't want to do. Speaking unkindly about yourself.

Farah lets her friends take food from her lunch box because she thinks it will make her more popular, even though it means she feels hungry all afternoon.

Aggressive: Trying to hide your low self-esteem by treating others in a bossy or unkind way.

Ben laughs loudly when other children make mistakes in class. He thinks making others feel bad will make him feel good.

Attention-seeking: Trying to get other people to tell you that you're a good or interesting person, trying to make people feel sorry for you, doing risky things so people pay attention to you.

Emily tells lies about herself and her family because she thinks this will make her more popular. She makes up dangerous and expensive activities she does at the weekend to tell her classmates.

Behaving in these ways might make you feel better for a little while, but in the long term they will make you feel worse, because they don't help to change the thoughts that make you feel bad, and your self-esteem doesn't get a chance to grow.

Avoidance behaviors

If you're like Rosie who stays at home to avoid activities, you aren't giving yourself a chance to find out what will really happen.

If you try, you have a chance at fun, success and learning. If you don't try, you'll never know, and your self-esteem can't grow.

Can you think of a time when you were really brave? Write or draw about it here:

How did it make you feel? Write or draw about it here:

Hiding behaviors

Yusuf thinks his friends will laugh at him if they find out he likes reading and writing poetry—is there something about yourself that you keep a secret? A true friend will respect you if you tell them about it, even if you are different from them in some way. It's the differences that make friendships interesting.

Can you think of a time you learned something surprising about a friend? Write or draw about it here:

How did you feel? Write or draw about it here:

You don't need to make a big announcement, you just need to choose to tell the truth when you get the chance to. Try practising what you might say, and using one of the relaxing exercises in the next chapter to help you say it calmly.

Perfectionist behaviors

Are you like Alex, who gets really tired trying to do everything perfectly, without asking for help? There is no such thing as perfect, so expecting to be perfect means you'll never be as good as you think you should be. To let your self-esteem grow, you need to give yourself a break and know that you can only do your best and no one expects more than that.

Can you think of a time you asked for help with something? Write or draw about it here:

What happened next? Write or draw about it here:

You can use steps (see pages 77–80) to change perfectionist behaviors too! Break down tasks into **realistic goals.** This means saying no to some things, and accepting that your best is good enough. If you don't achieve the steps exactly as you'd planned, that's OK.

Passive behaviors

Standing up for yourself can be scary. Sometimes it feels easier to let others get their way and keep your own feelings a secret, like Farah. But these behaviors make your self-esteem get lower and lower, because you start to believe that you aren't as important as other people. The answer is to learn how to be **assertive.**

Being assertive means being respectful to yourself and others. When someone is assertive they can think and make choices for themselves while also listening to others. You can use the thought-flipping skills you learned about on pages 65–67 to turn passive thoughts and behavior into assertiveness.

For example: Someone pushes in front of you in the lunch line at school

Passive thought	Passive behavior	Flip it!	Assertive thought	Assertive behavior
They probably deserve to eat their lunch first	Saying "sorry" and letting them go first	→	I was here first, and I deserve to eat my lunch just as much as they do	Saying "Excuse me, I was here first."

Can you think of a time you didn't stand up for yourself? Write or draw about it here:

What happened next? Write or draw about it here:

It's not always easy to plan when and where you'll have the chance to stand up for yourself, so it can be useful to practise and make promises to yourself. Think about the situation you just wrote about, but this time change the ending—imagine yourself acting assertively. You can do this in your head or act it out in front of the mirror. Then, when you get the chance to stand up for yourself, you'll know what to do. You might feel shy and it might feel strange, but you can use your new thought-challenging skills to help you do it anyway. Behaving assertively will lead to other people treating you better, and also boost your self-respect and self-esteem.

Write about your plan to behave assertively in the table on the following page:

Example:

If you don't know how to fill in the table, go to page 93

Passive thought	Passive behavior	Flip it!	Assertive thought	Assertive behavior
		↑		

Here are some other situations you could practise:

* Your friend tells you they don't like a TV show, but you do like it

* Your friend promised to sit next to you at lunch but it seems like they've forgotten their promise

* You are at the park and someone steals your ball

* A bully is being unkind to your friend

Here are some promises you can make to yourself:

* I will put my hand up in class when I know the answer

* I will speak up in a group discussion

* My feelings and thoughts are important and I can talk about them

* I can stand up for myself

* I can stand up for my friends

Aggressive behaviors

Ben tries to boss other children around to hide his low self-esteem. But making others feel bad is unkind and it doesn't help Ben to feel good—it actually hurts his self-esteem. We learned about **assertiveness** on page 93, and assertiveness is the way to change aggressive behaviors too!

When you feel like you're going to act in an aggressive way, take a breath and use your thought-flipping skills from pages 65–67 to turn your thoughts into assertive ones.

For example: Someone starts playing with your ball at the park

Aggressive thought	Aggressive behavior	Flip it!	Assertive thought	Assertive behavior
They did it on purpose!	Push and shout at them	→	Perhaps they made a mistake, I'll talk to them	Say, "Hey! That's my ball. Can I have it back please?"

★ Assertiveness means being respectful to yourself and others. When someone is assertive they can think and make choices for themselves while also listening to others.

When we are assertive, we think about other people's feelings and our own. Can you think of a time when you acted in an aggressive way? Write or draw about it here:

What happened next? How did you feel? Write or draw about it here:

Can you practise that situation again, but this time imagine what you might do if you were acting assertively and write it in the table below.

If you don't know how to fill in the table, go to page 99

Aggressive thought	Aggressive behavior	Flip it!	Assertive thought	Assertive behavior
		→		

Here are some other situations you might like to practise:

★ A friend shows you a mistake in a piece of writing you have done

★ You're trying out a new sport and can't get the hang of it

★ You're doing a group project at school and it's time to decide who will do which job

THIS IS HARD WORK, BUT I'M DOING SO WELL!

Attention-seeking behaviors

Like Emily, do you try to get people to look at you, feel sorry for you or say nice things about you to make yourself feel better? It can feel good to be the centre of attention, but if you have low self-esteem that feeling disappears once the attention is gone. Only you can make your self-esteem grow.

Can you think of any attention-seeking habits you have? Write or draw them here:

(For example, Emily's teacher was saying nice things about Emily's friend Anwar, and Emily felt a bit left out. So she started to complain loudly that her arm was hurting, so the teacher would pay attention to her instead.)

To change attention-seeking behavior, you need to slowly break these habits.

Note down each time you behave in an attention-seeking way in a week. Write what you did, and count up how often you did it—don't worry, you don't have to show this page to anyone.

Monday	
Tuesday	
Wednesday	
Thursday	
Friday	
Saturday	
Sunday	

You can change your behavior by taking control of these habits.

If you feel like you need to behave in an attention-seeking way, try doing something else for a few minutes before you do it. You could try:

★ Counting to 100

★ Singing your favorite song in your head

★ Trying to spot every color of the rainbow in the area around you

This will help you feel calmer, and you might find you don't feel like behaving in an attention-seeking way afterwards.

You can also set yourself a limit on how many times you can behave in an attention-seeking way each day. Take a look at the table on the previous page—can you cut the number of times you behave in an attention-seeking way in half next week?

If you want or need someone to pay attention to you, that's OK! You can ask for help or be proud of something you can do. Try to act **assertively** (find out more about this on page 93)—think of others as well as yourself, because everyone deserves attention just as much as you do.

If you can grow your self-esteem and cut down your attention-seeking behavior, you'll see that those around you will pay attention to you in a more positive way, and you won't feel so jealous when others are getting attention.

PART 4: LOOKING AFTER YOURSELF

Take time to chill

Growing your self-esteem is hard work, and you're doing brilliantly! We all feel tense or unhappy sometimes, and looking after yourself is a huge part of looking after your self-esteem.

Spend time doing what you love to do, rather than what other people think you should do. You are just as important as your friends and the other members of your family, so making time to relax and have fun with your friends, or just enjoy your own company is a good way to help you feel happy. Hiding away from your problems is never the answer so if you do want some time out, make it positive!

What is tension? What does it feel like?

Imagine you are holding something very small and very precious, like a gem stone. Clench your hands very tightly around it as hard as you can… now let go.

Did you feel your whole body change when you clenched your hands? That's tension. When you let go, that is relaxation.

When we feel upset or worried, we often feel tense. It's useful to learn some tricks to beat tension and help you relax.

ACTIVITY: TREE BREATHING

Breathe in, imagining your nose is the trunk of this tree. Let the air spread all the way up, into every branch until each bud bursts into blossom. Now breathe out, back down to the base of the tree. Do this five times. This tree breathing activity will help you feel calm and in control.

ACTIVITY: WHAT MAKES YOU FEEL RELAXED?

_____

_____

_____

_____

_____

_____

_____

_____

_____

_____

_____

_____

_____

_____

_____

_____

You could try one of these…

* Count how many kinds of leaf you can find in your garden

* Write a poem

* Re-read your favorite book

* Draw a self-portrait

* Write about your dream playground—what's in the playground? What can you hear? Smell? Feel? See?

* Paint a picture of the view from your window

* Sort small toys, beads or buttons into groups

* Listen to music

* Take a nap

* Look at some art

* Write a letter to someone special

* Stroke your pet

* Sing along with the radio

* Tell a funny joke

* Drink a tall glass of water through a straw

I AM
SPECIAL

ACTIVITY: THE BIG SCRIBBLE

Color in each gap—the only rule is you can't have two of the same color touching.

★ **You can do this activity anywhere! All you need to make your own is colored pencils and a piece of paper.**

Worry

If you have a worry chasing around and around in your head, let it out!

You could write it down if it's something you feel shy talking about, but it's amazing how much better you'll feel if you share your worry with someone you trust and talk about it. Together, you can work out how to solve the problem.

Why not write about your worries here, or in your diary from page 71?

Don't compare yourself to others

It's easy to see the best in our friends, but sometimes trickier to think kind thoughts about ourselves. **Talk to yourself in the same way you would talk to your best friend**. Remember, if someone can cycle faster, draw better or swim further than you, it's usually because they've had more practice. Take a break if you're feeling frustrated, but don't give up.

If you enjoy something, the fun you have when you are doing it is the important part. You don't need to be the best at everything!

But if there's an activity or hobby you love but can't do as well as you'd like, the best thing to do is more of it. Even Olympic champion swimmers had to start with the doggy paddle!

> ★ **Making mistakes means that you are trying, and we learn something new from each mistake we make.**

Be yourself

You're an absolute star: your family and friends love you because of your special and unique personality, so let yourself shine!

ACTIVITY: I AM BRILLIANT AT...

What are your skills? Everyone has things they're good at, and listing them will help you feel proud of yourself. Maybe you're a fast runner, tell the funniest jokes or are fantastic at coloring in. Write five things you can do well in the spaces below:

Now let's write down something you'd like to improve:

_____

_____

_____

_____

_____

_____

What could you do to improve this skill?

_____

_____

_____

_____

_____

_____

Now write down something you can't do **yet**:

_____

_____

_____

_____

_____

_____

How could you learn to do that?

_____

_____

_____

_____

_____

_____

Differences of opinion

Suppose the other children in your class all think cake is the best food, but you love ice cream. Who is right? Neither… and both! You don't have to think the same as everyone else. Friends don't have to agree on everything—in fact, it's much more interesting when people have different opinions.

No two human beings are exactly alike, even twins! We are all unique and special, and you'll have some things in common and some differences with each person you meet.

Don't be afraid to disagree… or to change your mind!

Can you think of something you've disagreed with a friend about?

_____

_____

_____

_____

_____

_____

Now think of something you've changed your mind about.

_____

_____

_____

_____

_____

_____

I WILL NOT CHANGE OR HIDE MYSELF TO FIT SOMEONE ELSE'S IDEA OF WHAT I SHOULD BE

ACTIVITY: I'M AN EXPERT!

Is there a subject you're an expert on? E.g., I know all about the Stone Age, or I'm a brilliant pet owner because… Draw or write about it here:

ACTIVITY: WHICH THREE WORDS WOULD YOUR BEST FRIEND USE TO DESCRIBE YOU?

Doesn't it feel good to remind yourself what's brilliant about you?

Feel great

Looking after your body is super important! There are lots of simple ways to keep healthy and take good care of your body.

ACTIVITY: HOW MANY TYPES OF EXERCISE DO YOU DO?

It doesn't need to be a sport—walking, playing tag, climbing trees and dancing are all types of exercise. Any time you're moving your body counts! Write as many as you can think of:

_____

_____

_____

_____

_____

_____

Draw yourself joining in with Bop!

* **Can you do one hour of exercise time each day? You can add it up like this:**

* **E.g., 15 minutes walking + 20 minutes playing tag + 25 minutes climbing trees = 1 hour**

Exercise doesn't just help keep your body healthy. When you exercise, special feel-good chemicals are released in your brain, helping you feel happy too!

Eat healthily

Treats like chocolate or crisps are nice occasionally, but eating plenty of delicious healthy food will make you feel good and give you loads of energy for doing the things you love.

ACTIVITY: WHAT ARE YOUR FAVORITE FRUIT AND VEGETABLES?

Draw a tower of the fruit and a tower of the vegetables that you like on the plates below—which is taller?

★ **Try to munch through five pieces of fruit or vegetables a day.**

Water is wonderful!

The human body is over 60 percent water, and we're constantly losing it—when we breathe out, when we sweat, cry or go to the bathroom.

Kids need at least six to eight drinks of water per day to stay healthy and hydrated. Drinking plenty of water helps you grow, play and learn.

Did you know?
* Since the beginning of time, there has always been the same amount of water on earth. It keeps being recycled, so the water we drink and wash with today is made of the same molecules drunk by dinosaurs!

ACTIVITY: MY BEDROOM

Being tired feels horrible! When you've had a good night's sleep you feel happier, and you can have more fun. What is your bedroom like? Can you draw it here?

My bedroom

> ★ **Try to get plenty of sleep every night**

If your bedroom is tidy and filled with things that are special and interesting to you, it'll be a relaxing and peaceful place to be. If your room is a bit cluttered, why not sort through your things and donate any toys you no longer play with to charity? You'll have more space to enjoy the toys and games you love.

ACTIVITY: A GOOD NIGHT'S SLEEP

Do you ever have trouble getting to sleep? Try this trick:

When you're in bed, get cosy under the covers and think about your ear lobes. How do they feel? How about your chin? Close your eyes and slowly check in on each little part of your body, from the top of your head to the soles of your feet. This will make you feel relaxed and sleepy.

Love your body

Your body is amazing. It is made up of 37 trillion cells, which all work together to keep you breathing, laughing, singing and dancing. Your heart beats over 100,000 times every day. Messages travel through your nerves to your brain at speeds of up to 170 miles per hour.

Your body changes as you get older and start to grow into an adult, which might make you feel worried or embarrassed—remember everyone experiences these changes, you're definitely not the only one.

It's common to feel shy about your body, so if you do feel shy, remember that no one but you is allowed to see or touch your body if you don't want them to. You can always talk to your parents or a trusted teacher about anything that's troubling you.

Mirror, mirror

Some people think being attractive is important but can attractiveness play tag? Can attractiveness share a midnight feast with you? Can attractiveness give you a hug when you're feeling down? No, only people each with their own wonderful and unique personalities can do those things.

Your body, your face, your smile… all of you from the hair on your head to the tips of your toenails is just right for you.

Remember: **you don't exist for other people to look at!** It's a gazillion times more important to focus on being happy than wasting time trying to please other people.

Planet Perfect

A lot of the people we see on TV and in magazines look like aliens from Planet Perfect, and it can sometimes affect your self-esteem if you don't look like they do. Did you know that special lights and computer tricks are used to make them look perfect? In real life famous people are just normal human beings, and the best and most interesting people are the ones who dress and present themselves in a way that's most comfortable to them.

If someone tries to make you feel bad because of how you look, it's not your body, face, clothes or hair that needs to change, it's their attitude.

If you're feeling down about how you look, remember that there is no such thing as perfect. Treat your body like a unique and precious treasure, because it is!

I am awesome

I am unique

ACTIVITY: I LIKE MYSELF!

Can you write or draw your three favorite things about your body? (Feel free to write more than three!) E.g., My curly hair, my strong legs, my big brain…

★ **Everyone has different parts of their body that they feel most confident about.**

PART 5: FUTURE PLANS

Looking to a bright future

The activities in this book will hopefully have helped you grow your self-esteem and given you some of the skills needed to keep it high. Well done! You have achieved a lot.

Now that you know all about self-esteem and understand how your thoughts and feelings work, you can use what you've learned every day.

Don't worry if your self-esteem still feels low sometimes, that's normal—you can always look again at this book, talk to an adult you trust or just take a break to relax.

ACTIVITY: MY FUTURE PLANS

What do you want to be when you grow up? There's more to this question than just a job. Draw a picture or write about how you'd like your life to be when you're an adult.

Where would you like to live? What will you do for fun? Will you have any pets?

You are not alone!

Most children feel down about themselves from time to time, and lots of children just like you have grown their self-esteem by being brave and changing how they think about themselves and the world around them.

Ruby, 8: "I was really worried about silly old sports day. I hated doing the races. I didn't want to do it because it was the worst thing at school in the world. FACT. But when I did the race it was over and it was fun cheering on our house team. Our team came second. Next year I won't be as worried."

Jack, 10: "Last year I had two best friends, but they often left me out. I used to think it was because I was boring, but now I have made new friends who don't leave me out, I don't think that any more."

Amena, 11: "I was bullied for a long time; the bullies told me I was fat and that I should hide myself away. For a while I thought they were right. Now I know that there is nothing wrong with my body, and that the bullies were wrong."

Callum, 9: "I got really angry with myself when I got a B in a test. My friend got a B too and was happy with his grade."

Phoebe, 8: "I feel nervous before acting in a school play or speaking in assembly, but when I'm doing it I enjoy myself."

Ali, 7: "I went to a birthday party and was sick afterwards, so I didn't go to any more birthday parties in case I was sick again. I went to my sister's party and I didn't get sick so I feel a bit better about it now."

Bethany, 11: "I feel so shy at school. All the other children are much cleverer than me, and I didn't used to put my hand up in class, in case I got the answer wrong. Maths is my favorite subject, so I feel more confident when we're doing maths and put my hand up more. I feel good when I try my best."

Ahmed, 11: "I have dyslexia so reading is hard for me. I didn't want my friends to know about my dyslexia, so I made fun of them if I saw them reading a book. Now my teacher has taught the class all about dyslexia I don't feel embarrassed about it anymore, and I don't need to make fun of my friends to feel better."

Tilly, 7: "When I got glasses I thought I looked silly and that my friends would laugh at me. I pretended to be ill so I didn't have to go to school. When I did go to school my friends thought my glasses looked really cool!"

The end!

Bop's had a great time learning all about self-esteem with you, have you enjoyed it too? You can come back to this book whenever you like to remind yourself about how self-esteem works, or look at all the cool activities you've completed.

You should be super proud of yourself for all the hard work you've done—goodbye and good luck, and remember: you're a star!

For parents: What you can do to help boost your child's self-esteem

The best thing you can do for your child's self-esteem is to set a good example. Talk kindly about yourself in front of your child, even if you think they aren't listening! They might not like to admit it sometimes, but you are your children's role model and they learn so much of how to be a grown-up from watching how you behave. Try not to focus on looks or what other people think, look after your own mental health and cultivate your own interests, to show them that you too are special and unique.

When faced with a problem, try to use positive, solutions-based language. If something's gone wrong, it's not immediately important to work out who's to blame or how it could have been avoided. Look at the situation carefully and work out how to make it right.

Show your child that you're still learning and trying new things even as an adult. If you're learning a new skill, show or tell them about your first attempt. Children understand abstract concepts best when we can give them real-life examples. So you could talk about how long it took to pass your driving test, or show them one of their baby photos, and talk about all the things they have learned to do since then.

Talk to your child about diversity and teach them how to show respect to others. If your child can appreciate difference in the people they meet, it will be easier for them to believe in their own specialness.

It can be tempting when your child is doubting their abilities to compliment and praise everything they do. But they'll get wise to this strategy very quickly! Instead, try to be specific with your praise—for example, if they've drawn a great picture, compliment their attention to detail or ask them about a particular part of the drawing. Take an interest in their interests, and they'll enjoy being the expert.

Conversely, if you know they're struggling or they aren't trying their best, suggest small ways they could improve or break the process into smaller steps.

Peer pressure can be powerful at this age, so let your child know that they are special and wonderful as they are. Try to gently encourage them towards positive role models, and feed their imagination with inspiring books, films and activities.

I really hope you've found the information and activities in this book helpful. It's always horrible when your child doesn't seem to see how wonderful they truly are, and you're doing a fantastic job by helping and supporting them in working through feelings of low self-esteem. On the next few pages there are suggestions for further advice and reading, so all that remains for me to do is to wish you the very best of luck!

Further advice

If you're worried about your child's mental health, do talk it through with your pediatrician or family doctor. While almost all children experience feelings of low self-esteem, some may need extra help. There are loads of great resources out there for information and guidance on children's mental health.

Recommended reading

··

Banish Your Self-Esteem Thief: A Cognitive Behavioral Therapy Workbook on Building Positive Self-Esteem for Young People
Kate Collins-Donnelly
Jessica Kingsley Publishers, 2014

The Story Cure: An A–Z of Books to Keep Kids Healthy, Happy and Wise
Ella Berthoud and Susan Elderkin
Canongate, 2016

Stand Up for Yourself & Your Friends: Dealing with Bullying and Bossiness, and Finding a Better Way
Patti Kelley Criswell
American Girl Publishing, 2016

Credits

··